Teach Your Dog

Jèrriais

Funny & surprisingly clever books. Love. Love.
DAWN FRENCH, ACTOR & COMEDIAN

Anne Cakebread not only has the best name in the Universe, she has also come up with a brilliantly fun book which will help humans and canines learn new languages.
RICHARD HERRING, COMEDIAN

I'm fed up with teaching my dogs all these different languages. It's like the Tower of Babel in here.
LUCY GANNON, WRITER

Just marvellous for all the wonderful dogs on our island to have a book they can read in their native language!
PETER JAMES, BESTSELLING CRIME AUTHOR

Teach Your Dog

JÈRRIAIS

Anne Cakebread

Thank you to:
Helen, Marcie, Fred and Wilma,
my family, friends and neighbours in
St Dogmaels for all their support and
encouragement, Carolyn at Y Lolfa and
Susan Parker for Jèrriais translations and
pronunciations.
Mèrcie bein des fais.

In memory of Frieda, who started us on
the *Teach Your Dog* journey.

First impression: 2023

© Anne Cakebread & Y Lolfa Cyf., 2023

This book is subject to copyright and may not be reproduced by any means except for review purposes without the prior written consent of the publishers.

Illustrations and design by Anne Cakebread

ISBN: 978-1-80099-443-0

Published and printed in Wales on paper from well-maintained forests by
Y Lolfa Cyf., Talybont, Ceredigion SY24 5HE
e-mail ylolfa@ylolfa.com
website www.ylolfa.com
tel 01970 832 304

*I grew up only speaking English.
When I moved to west Wales, I adopted Frieda,
a rescue whippet, who would only obey
Welsh commands.
Slowly, whilst dealing with Frieda, I realised that I was
overcoming my nerves about speaking Welsh aloud,
and my Welsh was improving as a result
– this gave me the idea of creating a series of books
to help others learn languages.
You don't even have to go abroad to practise.
If you haven't got a dog, any pet or soft toy will do:
just have fun learning and speaking a new language.*

– Anne Cakebread

"Hello"

"Bouônjour"

pron:
"B<u>won</u>-<u>zh</u>oor"

- 'o' as in 'h<u>o</u>t'
- almost silent 'n'
- 'zh' as in '<u>Zh</u>ivago'
- like the 'j' in 'bonjour' in French

"Come here"

"Vé-t-en ichîn"

pron:
"Veh-ton ee-sha<u>n</u>"

almost silent 'n'

"Stop!"

"Arrête!"

pron:
"Ah-rate!"

"Do you want a cuddle?"

"Veurs-tu qué j'té catinne?"

pron:

"Ver-too kuh <u>zh</u>-teh <u>cah</u>-teen?"

'zh' as in '<u>Z</u>hivago'

stress this syllable

"Catch!"

"Happe!"

pron:
"Hup!"

"Fetch!"

"Va qu'si!"

pron:
"Va kuh-see!"

'a' as in '<u>a</u>go'

"Leave it!"

"Laîsse-lé!"

pron:
"Lace-leh!"

"Sit!"

"Assied-té!"

pron:
"Ass-ee-eh-teh!"

"No!"

"Nânnîn!"

pron:
"Naw-neh!"

"Stay!"

"Reste ichîn!"

pron:
"Rest ee-shin!"

almost silent 'n'

"Bathtime"

"Au bain"

pron:
"Oh ba"

'a' as in 'm<u>a</u>n'

"Bedtime"

"Au liet"

pron:
"Oh yeh"

"Lunchtime"

"À la soupe"

pron:
"A la soup"

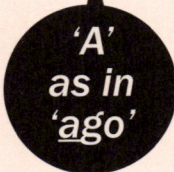

'A' as in 'ago'

"Are you full?"

"As-tu ieu assez à mangi?"

'A' as in '<u>a</u>go'

pron:

"<u>A</u> too yuh asseh a mon-<u>zh</u>ee?"

'zh' as in '<u>Zh</u>ivago'

"All gone"

"Tout finni"

pron:
"Too f<u>in</u>-nee"

'in'
as in
'b<u>in</u>'

"Good morning"

"Bouônjour à matîn"

pron:
"Bwon-zhoor a mat-in"

- 'a' as in 'ago'
- 'i' as in 'bin'
- almost silent 'n'

"Goodnight"

"Bouonne niet"

pron:
"Bwonn nee-eh"

"Don't scratch"

"N'té gratte pon"

pron:
"N-teh gr̃att pon"

- roll the 'r'
- 'o' as in 'hot'
- almost silent 'n'

"Let's go..."

"Cache..."

pron:
"C**u**sh..."

'u' as in '<u>u</u>p'

"Go down"

"À bas"

pron:
"A bah"

'A' as in 'ago'

"Up you go"

"À haut"

pron:
"<u>A</u> hoe"

'A' as in '<u>a</u>go'

"Go straight ahead"

"Tout drait"

pron:
"Too dreh"

"Go left"

"À la gauche"

pron:
"A la goe-sh"

- 'A' as in 'ago'
- 'oe' as in 'toe'

"Go right"

"À la drouaite"

pron:
"A la drwett"

'A' as in 'ago'

"Turn left"

"Touônne à la gauche"

pron:
"Twon <u>a</u> la g<u>oe</u>-sh"

- 'a' as in '<u>a</u>go'
- 'oe' as in 't<u>oe</u>'

"Turn right"

"Touônne à la drouaite"

pron:
"Twon a la drwett"

'a' as in 'ago'

"How's it going?"

"Comment qu'tu'es?"

pron:
"Commok-too-ay?"

"Do you want to play?"

"Veurs-tu jouer?"

pron:
"Ver-too zhway?"

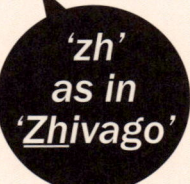

'zh' as in 'Zhivago'

"Lie down!"

"Couoche-té!"

pron:
"Kwosh-teh!"

'o' as in 'h<u>o</u>t'

"Say 'please'!"

"Di 's'i't'pliaît'!"

pron:
"Dee 'see-t-pee-ay'!"

"Can I have the ball?"

"J'peux-t-i' aver la balle?"

pron:

"*Zhuh-puh-tee aveh la bahl?*"

'Zh' as in 'Zhivago'

"Can I have a Jersey wonder?"

"J'peux-t-i' aver eune mèrvelle dé Jèrri?"

pron:

"Zhuh-puh-tee aveh urn mehr-vel deh Zheh-ree?"

'Zh' as in 'Zhivago'

"Very clever"

"Tu'es malîn"

pron:
"Too-ay mah-lin"

- 'i' as in 'b<u>i</u>n'
- almost silent 'n'

"It's warm"

"I' fait caud"

pron:
"Ee fay c<u>oe</u>"

'oe' as in 't<u>oe</u>'

"It's cold"

"I' fait fraid"

pron:
"Ee fay fray"

"The weather's nice"

"I' fait bieau temps"

pron:
"Ee fay by<u>oe</u> to<u>n</u>"

'oe' as in 't<u>oe</u>'

almost silent 'n'

"It's raining"

"I' tchait d'la plyie"

pron:
"Ee cheh dla pyee"

"Are you happy?"

"Es-tu heutheux?"

pron:
"Eh-too her-*thuh*?"

'th' as in '*this*'

"Who's snoring?"

"Tchi qu'est à ronflier?"

pron:

"Chee keh a ron-fee-yeh?"

- 'a' as in 'ago'
- almost silent 'n'

"Have you got enough room?"

"As-tu assez d'run?"

pron:

"A too asseh d-run?"

'A' as in 'ago'

almost silent 'n'

"See you soon"

"À la préchaine"

pron:
"A la preshen"

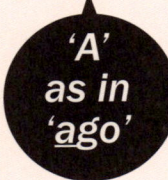

'A' as in 'ago'

"Be quiet!"

"Tai-té!"

pron:
"Tay-teh!"

"Who did that?"

"Tchi qu'a fait ch'na?"

pron:
"Chee kuh feh shnah?"

"There's a queue for the loo"

"I' y'a eune tcheue pouor la p'tite maîson"

pron:
"Ee ya urn chuh pwor la pteet mayson"

'a' as in 'ago'

'a' as in 'ago'

almost silent 'n'

1
"ieune"
pron: **"yern"**

2
"deux"
pron: **"d<u>uh</u>"**

'uh' as in 'h<u>uh</u>'

3
"trais"
pron:
"tray"

4
"quatre"
pron:
"kahtr"

soft 'r' from the throat

5
"chînq"
pron: **"shank"**

6
"six"
pron: **"see"**

"Thank you"

"Mèrcie bein des fais"

pron:
"Mehr-see ben day fay"

"Merry Christmas"

"Bouan Noué"

pron:
"Bwon Nweh"

"Congratulations!"

"Félicitâtions!"

pron:
"Fell-ee-see-tah-syon!"

almost silent 'n'

"Happy Birthday"

"Bouan Annivèrsaithe"

pron:
"*Bwon Annie-vair-sair<u>th</u>*"

'th' as in '<u>th</u>is'

"I love you"

"J't'aime"

pron:
"Zh-tem"

'Zh' as in '<u>Zh</u>ivago'

"Goodbye"

"À bétôt"

pron:
"A beh-toe"

'A' as in 'ago'